GROW YOUR MIND

BOOST

YOUR

BRAIN

Written by Alice Harman

Illustrated by David Broadbent

CRABTREE
PUBLISHING COMPANY
WWW.CRABTREEBOOKS.COM

CRABTREE
PUBLISHING COMPANY
WWW.CRABTREEBOOKS.COM

Author: Alice Harman
Series designer: David Broadbent
Illustrator: David Broadbent
Editor: Crystal Sikkens
Proofreader: Melissa Boyce
Print coordinator: Katherine Berti

A trusted adult is a person (over 18 years old) in a child's life who makes them feel safe, comfortable, and supported. It might be a parent, teacher, family friend, social worker, or another adult.

Library and Archives Canada Cataloguing in Publication

Title: Boost your brain / written by Alice Harman ; illustrated by David Broadbent.
Names: Harman, Alice, author. | Broadbent, David, 1977- illustrator.
Description: Series statement: Grow your mind | Includes index. | First published in Great Britain in 2020 by the Watts Publishing Group.
Identifiers: Canadiana (print) 2020021988X | Canadiana (ebook) 20200219936 | ISBN 9780778781660 (hardcover) | ISBN 9780778781745 (softcover) | ISBN 9781427125927 (HTML)
Subjects: LCSH: Brain—Care and hygiene—Juvenile literature. | LCSH: Brain—Growth—Juvenile literature. | LCSH: Mental health—Juvenile literature. | LCSH: Thought and thinking—Juvenile literature.
Classification: LCC QP376 .H37 2021 | DDC j612.8/2—dc23

Library of Congress Cataloging-in-Publication Data

Names: Harman, Alice, author. | Broadbent, David, 1977- illustrator.
Title: Boost your brain / written by Alice Harman ; illustrated by David Broadbent.
Description: New York : Crabtree Publishing Company, 2021. | Series: Grow your mind | Includes index.
Identifiers: LCCN 2020014727 (print) | LCCN 2020014728 (ebook) | ISBN 9780778781660 (hardcover) | ISBN 9780778781745 (paperback) | ISBN 9781427125927 (ebook)
Subjects: LCSH: Mental efficiency--Juvenile literature. | Intellect--Juvenile literature. | Brain--Juvenile literature.
Classification: LCC BF431 .H34195 2021 (print) | LCC BF431 (ebook) | DDC 155.4/191--dc23
LC record available at https://lccn.loc.gov/2020014727
LC ebook record available at https://lccn.loc.gov/2020014728

Crabtree Publishing Company

www.crabtreebooks.com   1-800-387-7650
Published by Crabtree Publishing Company in 2021

Published in Canada
Crabtree Publishing
616 Welland Ave.
St. Catharines, Ontario
L2M 5V6

Published in the United States
Crabtree Publishing
347 Fifth Ave.
Suite 1402-145
New York, NY 10116

Printed in the U.S.A./082020/CG20200601

First published in Great Britain in 2020 by The Watts Publishing Group Copyright © The Watts Publishing Group 2020

CONTENTS

A brain-boosting mindset

"I'm not smart enough to do that, there's no point trying."

"Argh, I just don't understand this! I'll never get it."

"Everything's easy for her because she's smarter than me."

Have you ever had any of these thoughts? How did they make you feel? Not great, right?

Sometimes we think about our brains as if they are stuck one way forever. We believe we can either do something or we can't, we're either smart or we're not. This way of thinking is known as a **fixed mindset**, and none of it is true!

The best way to boost our brains is to develop a **growth mindset**. This means understanding that the brain is never fixed as it is. We always have the power to make it change and grow.

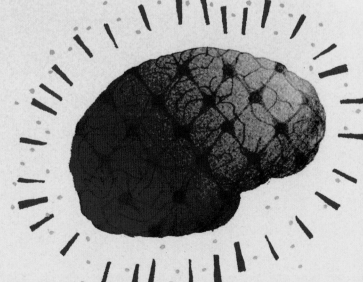

Let's look inside a brain to see exactly what we're talking about. Your brain has billions of **neurons** that pass information to each other. You are born with all these neurons, but they aren't all connected yet.

As you learn new things, neurons build bridges by zipping messages back and forth. The more you learn and practice, the stronger those bridges get. The more bridges you build, the more neurons there are to team up for maximum brain power!

This book has all kinds of fun ways to help you learn how to develop a growth mindset and boost your brain.

So let's get started!

Learning connects your neurons!

Sshhhhhhh...

Friends trying to talk to you, thoughts popping into your head, situations you can't help worrying about... Do you ever feel like your brain is so crowded with thoughts and noises that you just can't think properly?

Well, you're right! It's really hard for your brain to do its best work when it's so distracted and overloaded by all these other things.

You can boost your brain power by finding ways to take away these distractions, so you have a clear mind to focus on whatever you're trying to do.

Jamal

I was finding it really hard to concentrate in class. My friends kept talking to me when I was trying to listen or do my work.

It felt like there wasn't enough time to think in between people distracting me, so I was struggling to understand things.

I talked to my dad about it. We decided that I would tell my friends that although I loved talking to them, I needed to stop talking in class so I could focus more on my work.

They were really nice about it, but my friend Anna kept forgetting. I had to remind her to please stop talking to me in class, and that was really hard! But now I feel much happier and we're all still really good friends!

One thing at a time

Do you feel your mind wandering when you're trying to concentrate? Are you thinking about what you're going to have for dinner, what you're doing on the weekend, or what the words are to your new favorite song?

Even without people distracting you, it can be really tricky to focus on one thing for a long time—or even for a short time!

Your brain needs to concentrate on new challenges to make connections and grow, so how can you help it?

Well, just like a weight lifter strengthens their muscles over time, you can boost your brain by building up its concentration power bit by bit.

Try

Find an apple, then start a timer for 30 seconds and stare at the apple until the timer beeps. Try not to think about anything else but this apple during that time. It's harder than you think!

Think

How did that go? You may have found that other thoughts popped into your head and that's completely normal. When this happens, it can be helpful to say to yourself, "Oh, there's a thought!" and then imagine pushing it away gently, so it floats off like a balloon. You can also try focusing on counting to four as you breathe in, and then again as you breathe out. Silently saying "apple" over and over again to yourself is another trick to try.

Practice

Try it for 30 seconds again tomorrow. Then, in a notebook, write down the date, the length of time—"30 seconds," and a couple of lines about how it went. The next day, try 40 seconds, then 50, and so on. At the end of two weeks, look back and see how you've progressed and what you found that helped you focus best—you're the expert on your own brain!

Think, rest, repeat

We all want to do our best, but sometimes we need to remember that we are human beings, not machines.

Human beings can't keep working at top speed with maximum focus forever—our brains need a break!

If you've been working on something for a long time and you're getting frustrated because it's not going as well as you'd like, take a break. It's very hard for your brain to do its best thinking and growing when it's tired.

Taking regular rest breaks will boost your brain, leaving it happy and ready to learn for longer periods of time.

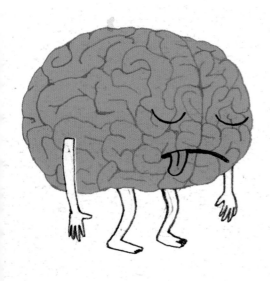

The next time you have a big project or a lot of homework to do, try splitting it up into sections with breaks in between.

Set a timer for 15 minutes when you start one section of work.

When it goes off, set the timer again for five minutes and take a break. During each break, think of a different way to do these three things:

1. Move around

2. Make yourself smile

3. Say something nice to yourself

When the break timer goes off, start the next section of work and set the timer again.

After three five-minute breaks, if you really need to keep working, give yourself a longer break.

Brain hugs

Do you ever say horrible, mean things to yourself that you'd never dream of saying to your friends?

Sometimes we can be really hard on ourselves, and it hurts our brains when we think like this. It stops them from doing their best learning and growing.

Think about it like this: if someone was really mean to you, and told you there was no point in trying because you wouldn't do it right anyway, would you still want to try? Probably not.

So we need to learn how to turn these mean, negative thoughts into friendly, positive **brain hugs**!

Jess

When I started playing soccer I really liked it, but after a while I felt like everyone else was better than me and it made me really upset.

I told myself that no one wanted me there, that I was no good, and I was ruining it for everyone else. I was thinking about quitting, even though it was still fun.

I talked to my uncle about it and he was really shocked. He thought I was so brave for joining the team even though I didn't know anyone there, and it sounded like I was learning a lot.

The next time I went to soccer, I tried to remember these positive things and it made me feel so much better. Now I'm really enjoying it again, and getting better all the time. Whenever I start feeling bad, I just give myself a "brain hug" and it really helps!

Time-out

When we get really worried, angry, confused, or frustrated, it can feel like we're trapped in that feeling and nothing can change that.

We might do things that we know aren't right and will make us feel bad later, such as cheating on a test or being mean to a friend we think has everything easy.

At these times, the best way to make a good decision is to give your brain a chance to calm down first. Take a time-out, breathe, and try to get yourself back in the right frame of mind to handle whatever is going on.

1.
Everyone's brain works a little differently, so let's create a **mind map** with the best ways to help yours calm down when you feel stuck or panicky.

2.
Draw your brain in the middle of a piece of paper. Add the different things that help you feel calm. They could be counting to 100, taking some deep breaths, or maybe remembering a happy time.

4.
Practice the different time-outs on your mind map, so you can remember them easily when you need them.

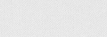

3.
Ask your family and friends what helps them to calm down, and maybe try out some of these ideas. If they work for you, add them to your mind map.

Take care of your body

Your brain is a funny and special thing because it's your mind and your body at the same time!

Sometimes we think about the "mind" side of our brain so much, such as our thoughts and feelings, that we forget to take care of the "body" side of it.

You can boost your brain by taking care of yourself in simple ways every day:

Drink up

Your brain cells need the right balance of water. If you get too thirsty, they don't work as well.

Get moving

Your brain loves exercise and you should do an hour of it every day. When your heart beats faster from running, jumping, swimming, and so on, it sends more oxygen to your brain and gives it a big boost.

Brain food

Stay healthy and boost your brain by eating a rainbow of different-colored fresh foods, including berries, beans, apples, and plums. Avoid too many sweets and sugary drinks. After a rush of energy, these sweets will cause you to have a sugar crash, which makes your body and brain suddenly feel tired.

Sleep tight

Try to get nine to twelve hours of sleep every night, or your brain will be tired and you'll feel it! If you have to get up early for school, count back the hours from when you have to wake up, to make sure you get to bed early enough.

BRAIN DUMP

Does your brain ever feel completely overloaded with all the different things you have to remember? Does it feel like there's no space left in it to think?

You can boost your brain by using a notebook to unload some of the thoughts it's trying to juggle. This frees up your brain to focus all its power on what it's doing at that moment.

We ask a LOT of our brains every day. It can be like trying to juggle many balls at the same time—we're so busy trying not to let anything fall that we can't do anything else. And it really drains our energy through the day.

Ask an adult to help you write a schedule
in a notebook of what you do every day,
such as school, activities, clubs, and so on.

Write reminders in your schedule for anything that
you need to remember to do at certain times—
for example, pack your schoolbag in the morning.

Carry this notebook with you so you can always check it.
When something comes up that you need to remember
to do, such as give your parents or guardians a letter
from school, write it down.

Pick a time every evening where you take 15 minutes to look
over what you wrote down that day and what's coming up in
the day ahead. If there are any changes to your schedule,
add a sticky note to remind yourself.

PICTURE THIS

Have you ever felt like you knew or understood something, but then it disappeared out of your brain or stopped making sense later on? Don't worry, it's frustrating but it happens to everyone!

One thing that can really help with remembering new information is to visualize it. That means creating a picture in your mind of what you've just learned.

You can then draw that picture and keep it to look at later, along with notes you've written down. You could even try testing yourself by recreating the picture in your mind at a later date and then trying to draw it again. Compare it to the original drawing. How much did you remember?

Rekah

I felt really frustrated at school because I just couldn't remember things! I understood the lessons, but as soon as I learned them it felt like the facts fell out of my brain just like water through a sieve.

I told my teacher and she suggested that I try visualizing things as I learned them. I gave it a try that evening with my homework as I learned about different types of animals.

I learned that amphibians, such as frogs, are cold-blooded and live in water and on land. To remember this, I pictured a cold, shivering frog half-in and half-out of a pond.

In class the next day, my teacher asked us about amphibians. I pictured the cold, shivering frog in my mind and told her all the facts I remembered. She was so happy that I tried out a new way to boost my brain!

SUM IT UP

When you get to the end of a project or task, it can be tempting to want to take a well-deserved rest. And no one is saying you shouldn't! But before you do, give your brain a boost!

Spend one minute thinking about what you've just done. It can help you better understand how your brain works, and recognize patterns that might be causing you problems.

What did you learn?

How difficult did you find it?

How much effort did you put into it?

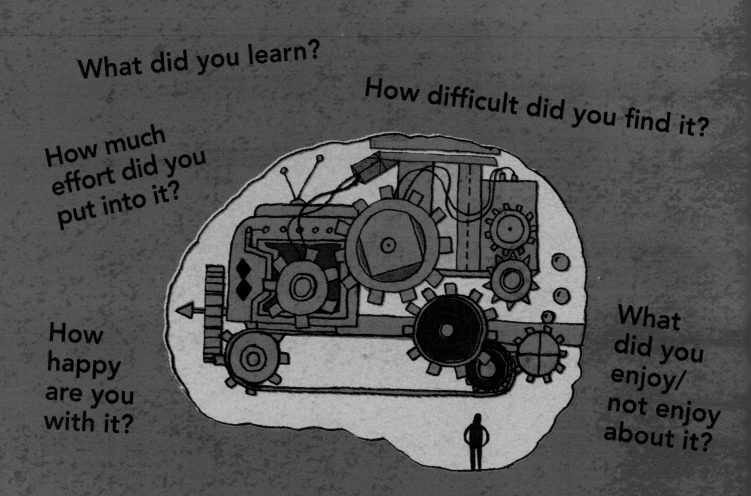

How happy are you with it?

What did you enjoy/ not enjoy about it?

What would you do differently next time?

Read through the questions on the previous page again.

Next time you finish a task or project, imagine that a crowd of news reporters is asking you all about it. Record yourself giving answers to all their questions.

One of the news reporters wants to film a full-length story all about you, so now they're following you around all week! Film yourself answering the same questions after every task or project you complete.

At the end of the week, watch the videos and make note of what you've said. Does anything keep coming up in each video?

Make a video finale where you talk about what you've learned and how you're going to try to work on any challenges.

Make a mnemonic

Boosting your brain doesn't have to be super-serious—it can be a lot of silly fun! One of the best ways to remember things is to make **mnemonics** (nuh-mon-ics).

That looks like a tricky word, doesn't it? But all it means is a way to help you remember information. You can use a mnemonic for anything, from science to spelling. Mnemonics can come in many forms, such as patterns of letters or numbers, rhymes, jokes, or songs.

Mnemonics that are funny or related to your life are the easiest to remember. Why not try making one right now for a word you find tricky to spell, such as mnemonics? One example for this word could be **M**y **N**eighbor **E**d **M**akes **O**dd, **N**ot **I**nteresting **C**at **S**ongs.

Marek

I love writing stories, but I find spelling is hard.
I used to hate seeing the spelling mistakes I made
when my teacher marked my work. It almost made
me want to stop writing stories all together.

I asked my dad how he remembered how to spell so many words.
He told me that when he got stuck on a word, he liked to use
a fun saying or a silly song to help him remember.

He shared one with me that he used for the word "because."
It went **Big Elephants Can Always Understand Small Elephants.**
He told me to picture little elephants talking and big elephants
nodding along. Then we practiced writing down the word
with its correct spelling. It worked!

We've come up with other mnemonics for all kinds of words—
sometimes we even make up songs! It's really helped me feel
more confident with my spelling and writing.

Also, it's fun!

STUDY BUDDIES

Have you ever felt bad because you thought someone else was smarter than you? Have you felt good when you thought you were smarter than someone else?

Tests and competitions can sometimes make us feel like we're only doing well if we're beating everyone else, but this isn't right at all.

Wanting to prove we're the smartest can make us scared to make mistakes or ask for help. Feeling like we're not the smartest can stop us from wanting to try at all. Either way, it's not helpful for your brain!

Instead of competing against people, try boosting your brain by working together with others and learning from them.

Ask someone in your class to partner up with you on a project or to be study buddies in a subject that you are finding difficult.

Pick regular times to meet and work together. At the end of each study session, tell each other:

★ **one way you feel you're trying hard and improving;**

★ **one way you can see them trying hard and improving;**

★ **one thing you've learned from them.**

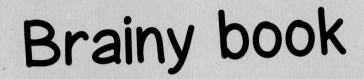

Brainy book

Everyone's brain is different and that's what makes the world interesting!

You're the world's greatest expert when it comes to your brain. You're going to be together for your whole life, so it's a good idea to get to know what keeps it growing and happy.

You may find that some of the ideas and activities in this book work really well for you, but others may not be helpful at all.
That's OK!

Turn a notebook into your own Brain Booster Journal. Use it to keep practicing the activities in this book that work well for you, and try out some new ideas of your own!

Keep track of your progress, so if you ever feel frustrated you can look back at your journal and see how far you've come and how much you've learned.

Remember that your brain needs time to change and grow. It might take a while before your new habits and ways of thinking feel natural, but if you keep putting in the effort, you will see the results.

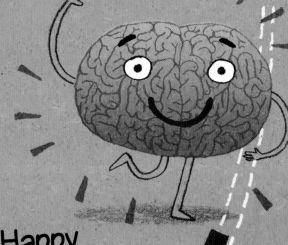

Happy brain boosting!

KEEP BOOSTING YOUR BRAIN!

Read through this book's brain-boosting tips any time you need a quick reminder!

Try to remove distractions that stop your
brain from being able to focus properly.

Practice thinking about one thing at a time
to help build up your concentration power.

Give yourself regular rest breaks to keep your brain happy and working well.

Turn negative, mean thoughts about yourself into friendly, positive "brain hugs."

Work out what calms down your brain when you feel stuck and panicky.

Take care of your brain by getting plenty of sleep,
exercising, eating healthy foods, and drinking water.

Free up some thinking space in your brain by
writing down plans, reminders, and things to do.

Visualize new information as you
learn it to help it stick in your brain.

Think about how you work and learn
so you know what works best for you.

Try making up mnemonics to help you remember
how to spell words or other pieces of information.

Work with others and learn from them
rather than competing against them.

Become an expert in what makes
your brain work best and be happiest.

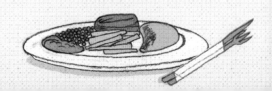

Glossary

brain hug   When you turn a nasty, negative thought about yourself into a positive, caring one that helps you and your brain feel better

fixed mindset   If you are using a fixed mindset, you believe that your intelligence is fixed and can't be changed

growth mindset   If you are using a growth mindset, you believe that your intelligence is always changing because your brain can grow stronger

mind map   A diagram with lines and circles for organizing information so that it is easier to remember

mnemonic   A rhyme, joke, or saying that helps a person remember something, from how to spell a word to the planets in our solar system

neurons   Cells in your brain that pass information back and forth to each other

Index

Notes for adults

The concept of a "growth mindset" was developed by psychologist Carol Dweck, and is used to describe a way in which effective learners view themselves as being on a constant journey to develop their intelligence. This is supported by studies showing how our brains continue to develop throughout our lives, rather than intelligence and ability being static.

Responding with a growth mindset means being eager to learn more and seeing that making mistakes and getting feedback about how to improve are important parts of that journey.

A growth mindset is at one end of a continuum, and learners move between this and a "fixed mindset"—which is based on the belief that you're either smart or you're not.

A fixed mindset is unhelpful because it can make learners feel they need to "prove" rather than develop their intelligence. They may avoid challenges, not wanting to risk failing at anything, and this reluctance to make mistakes—and learn from them—can negatively affect the learning process.

Help children develop a growth mindset by:

• Giving specific positive feedback on their learning efforts, such as "Well done, you've been practicing…" rather than non-specific praise, such as "Good effort" or comments such as "Smart girl/boy!" that can encourage fixed-mindset thinking.

• Sharing times when you have had to persevere learning something new and what helped you succeed.

• Encouraging them to keep a learning journal, where they can explore what they learned from new challenges and experiences.

• Exploring the science behind how our brains work and change, watching online video clips that show the brain in neuron-firing action.